BINDING TERMS

A Thesaurus for Use in

Rare Book and Special Collections Cataloguing

Prepared by the
Standards Committee
of the
Rare Books and Manuscripts Section
(ACRL/ALA)

Chicago
Association of College and Research Libraries
1988

The Library of Congress has assigned the following code to this thesaurus:

rbbin

This code must be entered in subfield ≠2 of USMARC field 755 when terms from this thesaurus are used in that field.

Published by the Association of College and Research Libraries, a division of the American Library Association, 50 East Huron Street, Chicago, IL 60611.

The paper used in this publication meets the minimum requirements of American National Standard for Information Sciences--Permanence of Paper for Printed Library Materials, ANSI Z39.48-1984∞.

ISBN 0-8389-7210-1

Printed in the United States of America.

ACKNOWLEDGEMENTS

The cover illustration, by Jost Amman, is taken from the Pierpont Morgan Library's copy of Hartmann Schopper's *Panoplia omnium illiberalium mechanicarum aut sedentiarium artium genera.* Frankfurt, 1568 (PML 76069). We are grateful to the library for permission to reproduce it. Some scope notes in this thesaurus are in the form of quotes. They have been taken from Paul Needham's *Twelve centuries of bookbindings 400-1600.* We are grateful to Mr. Needham and to the publisher, the Pierpont Morgan Library, for permission to use these quotes. We would also like to thank Paul Johnson and Bob Bassett, both of the University of Texas at Austin, for their help in editing this thesaurus and preparing it for the press.

BINDING TERMS
A Thesaurus for Use in
Rare Book and Special Collections Cataloguing

Introduction

I. History

The Independent Research Libraries Association (IRLA)'s *Proposals for Establishing Standards for the Cataloguing of Rare Books and Specialized Research Materials in Machine-readable Form* (Worcester, Mass., 1979) called for a new field to be added to machine-readable cataloguing (MARC) formats for terms indicating the physical characteristics of materials catalogued (Proposal Five), including descriptions of the bindings. In the same proposal IRLA requested that the Standards Committee of the Rare Books and Manuscripts Section of ACRL work toward developing standard terminology for use in such a field. The RBMS Standards Committee undertook the development of a thesaurus of terms, and a field for such terms (755 "Physical Characteristics Access") was authorized for all MARC formats in January 1984.

In order to expedite publication of the thesaurus, the RBMS Standards Committee decided to divide it into several separate thesauri, each treating evidence of a different aspect of book production and history. *Printing & Publishing Evidence: Thesauri for Use in Rare Book and Special Collections Cataloguing* has been published already by the committee. Further thesauri covering other aspects of book production and history, such as paper and papermaking, provenance, and type evidence are in draft form or are planned.

The present list presents terms for the description of bookbindings and includes descriptors relating to techniques for binding construction, and to the style, materials, and decoration of bindings. All but the broadest categories of tools have been excluded. The terms in the thesaurus come from drafts of the IRLA proposals, some existing lists in rare book libraries, various reference works, and comments on drafts of the list by individuals at several institutions. Major drafts of the thesaurus were prepared by Anna Lou Ashby and John D. Thomas, III, based on early work by Alexandra Mason and Patrick Russell.

II. Purpose and Scope

Many rare book libraries, concerned with the study of the book, maintain local files recording examples of various physical characteristics of items found in their collections. These files are used to retrieve books by physical features rather than by intellectual content. Although such files are useful for selection of materials for exhibition, for class demonstration, and for cataloguing comparison, their primary use is to assist researchers interested in studying the physical characteristics of books as evidence for their production, distribution, or further history. Reflecting for the most part local rather than standard cataloguing practices, such files have often remained available only within individual libraries. Developed specifically for use in MARC field 755, the following thesaurus provides standard terms for the retrieval of binding evidence. Such standardization is a necessity for those institutions working in the context of shared, machine-readable cataloguing but may also prove beneficial to those maintaining in-house files.

III. Form

This thesaurus consists of an alphabetical list of terms followed by a hierarchical arrangement of terms. Following ANSI standards (American National Standards Institute, *American National Standard Guidelines for Thesaurus Structure, Construction, and Use*, New York, 1980), the terms are in plural natural language noun form whenever possible, and in direct order. Although all terms are specific, an attempt has been made to include both genus of evidence (e.g., Waste) and species (e.g., Manuscript waste, Printed waste) in a number of cases.

The alphabetical list contains authorized terms and cross-references. Scope notes follow terms thought to be obscure or ambiguous or which are to be used in a technical sense. Each term is followed by the references, if any, made to and from other terms in the thesaurus. Symbols used in these references are those which ANSI prescribes:

USE   leads from unused synonyms and inverted forms of the terms to the
       term used,

UF   (used for) is the reciprocal of the USE reference and accompanies the
       term to which the USE reference refers;

BT   (broader term) refers from a term for a member of a class to the term
       for the class;

NT   (narrower term) refers from a term for a class to the term for one
       of its members;

RT   (related term) is used between related terms when it seems helpful
       to bring associated types of evidence to the user's attention.

In the present thesaurus, members of a class related to each other as narrower terms (NTs) under a common class (BT) are not related to each other as related terms (RTs). Whenever a term for which there are narrower terms in the thesaurus appears under another term as either a narrower term (NT) or a related term (RT), it is followed by the symbol ">" to indicate that it is not the narrowest concept of its class. Users should consult the entry for terms so marked to identify narrower terms.

In keeping with ANSI standards, this thesaurus also includes a hierarchical section which displays graphically the relationships between broader and narrower terms. In order to bring together terms relating to the same aspect of the subject, the hierarchy contains several gathering terms (displayed within square brackets), which serve to arrange the hierarchical relationship; these terms are not authorized for use in field 755 and do not appear in the alphabetical list.

A binding is fundamentally a structure, whose materials and techniques of construction influence its appearance, while not excluding the further decorative elaboration of the result; indeed, the "style" of bindings has traditionally been the aspect of most interest to collectors. To reflect this situation, the hierarchical arrangement of binding terms is divided into groups which progress from description of the text block, type of binding structure and its parts, to materials and their treatment, categories and styles of bindings, and miscellaneous evidence about bindings. A number of the terms in the list can be regarded as describing either the material of the binding and its treatment, or, alternatively, the decorative style of the result, or the category or occasion of the binding. For example, "Mottled calf bindings" can be viewed as an example of material and treatment, or of style; "Printed boards" or "Pictorial cloth bindings", while describing the material and its treatment, apply to categories of bindings produced by publishers. In all the instances where such ambiguity occurs, the hierarchy classifies the term under its material or functional aspect, which is not intended to preclude its use by those interested in the style of the binding or the occasion of its production. One term occurring in the alphabetical list is not found in the hierarchical display: the term "Bookbinding" is provided for use with subdivisions to allow for identifications and classifications not provided by the terms in the present list.

IV. Application

In a MARC record, these terms are to be entered in subfield $\neq$a ("access term") of field 755. Terms which do not appear in this or other thesauri approved for field 755 may not be used in this field. When used in a MARC record, a parenthetical qualifier must be added in subfield $\neq$a following the term. The qualifier will aid users who may not see or know how to interpret the coding for subfield $\neq$2 (see below), and it also helps clarify terms which are ambiguous when taken out of context (e.g., "Washing" or "Silk ties"). Terms from the present list receive the qualifier "(Binding)" even when the approved term itself ends with the word "bindings" When the thesaurus term has a specific parenthetical qualifier, the general qualifier follows the specific qualifier within a separate set of parentheses.

Any term in this thesaurus may be subdivided by place ($\neq$z), period ($\neq$y), or other subdivision ($\neq$x), or by any combination of these subdivisions. Each library must determine its own scheme for chronological subdivision. Indirect subdivision, as outlined in LC's *Cataloging Service Bulletin* 120 (1977), p. 9-11, is to be used when subdividing by place. Libraries using other subdivisions ($\neq$x) should construct these subdivisions to conform as far as possible to LC practice as defined in publications such as *Library of Congress Subject Headings: A Guide to Subdivision Practice* (Washington, 1981) or *Cataloging Service Bulletin*.

Each 755 field must close with a subfield $\neq$2 ("source of access term"). The Library of Congress has assigned the code "rbbin" to the present thesaurus. Therefore, 755 fields using terms from the list of binding terms must close with "$\neq$2 rbbin".

Examples of the application of subdivided terms:

> 755   Armorial bindings (Binding) $\neq$z France $\neq$y 18th century. $\neq$2 rbbin

> 755   Centerpieces (Designs) (Binding) $\neq$z England $\neq$y 17th century. $\neq$2 rbbin

N.B.: Subfields $\neq$a (with qualifier) and $\neq$2 are mandatory, other subfields are optional.

Field 755 is repeatable; assign as many terms as appropriate and desirable to retrieve types of evidence in an item. For example, a binding described as "Olive morocco over wooden boards, gold-tooled, inlays of light brown, dark brown, and reddish-brown morocco; black paint; remains of four pairs of braided clasps; edges gilt" (Paul Needham, *Twelve Centuries of Bookbindings: 400-1600* (New York, 1979), no. 58) could have any or all of these 755s: "Greek style bindings", "Morocco bindings", "Wooden boards", "Gold tooled bindings", "Inlays", "Painted bindings" (or "Painted leather bindings"), "Clasps", and "Gilt edges".

Use of field 755 is voluntary. Some libraries may want to use the field only for several of the terms; other libraries may prefer to use none. In the case of those terms linked by a genus-species relationship, some libraries may wish to use only the broader term; other libraries may prefer to assign only the narrower terms when appropriate, saving the broader term for items not covered by any narrower terms in the thesaurus. The thesaurus of binding terms is designed to create special files in a library of any size, whether it has only a few unusual bindings that might be identified for teaching or exhibition purposes, or a large collection in which particular characteristics are kept track of systematically. A small file is more likely to consist of general terms, while a large one will probably contain many more specific terms, but these decisions should be based on the institution's needs.

Descriptions of bindings are for the most part copy-specific; even in the case of publishers' and edition bindings, variants often occur which frequently constitute the principal points of interest for those studying the bindings. Libraries doing original cataloguing should describe as desired the physical characteristics of their own copies; other libraries making later use of such cataloguing will need to evaluate the 755 entries for appropriateness to their own copies.

These terms are to be used in field 755 regardless of the appearance of the same information elsewhere in the record (such as in a subject heading or in a note), their primary purpose being to provide easy retrieval of examples of binding characteristics through a single source.

Most of the history and description of bookbinding has been published in the form of descriptions, usually with illustrations, of specific bindings or of the bindings in specific collections. Consequently, a thorough search of the literature entails the examination of many volumes of narrow scope. The following list of titles includes only a small group of works containing information of a general nature. The descriptions, illustrations, and bibliographies found in them serve as useful starting points from which to approach the questions of style, period, and technique.

Carter, John. *ABC for Book Collectors.* London: Rupert Hart-Davis, 1952. Also available in many revised English and American editions.

Carter, John. *Binding Variants in English Publishing, 1820-1900.* London: Constable & Co.; New York: Ray Long & Richard R. Smith, 1932.

Diehl, Edith. *Bookbinding: Its Background and Technique.* New York: Rinehard & Company, 1946. 2 vols. Reprinted, New York: Dover Publications, 1980.

English Bindings 1490-1940 in the Library of J.R. Abbey. Ed. G. D. Hobson. London: Privately printed at the Chiswick Press, 1940.

The History of Bookbinding, 525-1950 A.D. An exhibition held at the Baltimore Museum of Art November 12, 1957 to January 12, 1958. Ed. Dorothy Miner. Baltimore: The Walters Art Gallery, 1957.

Middleton, Bernard C. *A History of English Craft Bookbinding Technique.* New York & London: Hafner Publishing Company, 1963. Supplemented 2nd ed., London: Holland Press, 1978.

Needham, Paul. *Twelve Centuries of Bookbindings, 400-1600.* New York: The Pierpont Morgan Library; London: Oxford University Press, 1979.

Nixon, Howard M. *Broxbourne Library: Styles and Designs of Bookbindings from the Twelfth to the Twentieth Century.* London: Published for the Broxbourne Library by Maggs Brothers, 1956.

Nixon, Howard M. *Five Centuries of English Bookbinding.* London: Scolar Press, 1978.

Roberts, Matt T., and Don Etherington. *Bookbinding and the Conservation of Books: A Dictionary of Descriptive Terminology.* Washington, D.C.: Library of Congress, 1982.

Sadleir, Michael. *The Evolution of Publishers' Binding Styles, 1770-1900.* London: Constable & Co.; New York: Richard R. Smith, 1930.

V. Revision

The RBMS Standards Committee is responsible for the maintenance and revision of this thesaurus. It solicits suggestions for new terms, corrections, and alterations to terms, scope notes, and references. Any new term proposed should be accompanied by a scope note and references if appropriate. Any correspondence regarding this thesaurus should be addressed to

Chair, Standards Committee
Rare Books and Manuscripts Section
ACRL/ALA
50 East Huron Street
Chicago, IL 60611

Attention: Binding Terms

RBMS Standards Committee Members, 1985-1987

Anna Lou S. Ashby
Helen S. Butz
Dianne M. Chilmonczyk
Michèle V. Cloonan
Alan N. Degutis
Jackie M. Dooley
Peter S. Graham
Rebecca R. Hayne

Paul S. Koda
Sara Shatford Layne
Hope Mayo
Elisabeth Betz Parker
Judith C. Singleton
Joseph A. Springer
John B. Thomas, III

BINDING TERMS

Accordion fold format
  UF   Double leaf format
        Orihon format

Adhesive bindings
  UF   Perfect bindings
  NT   Caoutchouc bindings
  RT   Non-adhesive bindings

All along sewing
  RT   Two-on sewing

All-over style bindings

Alum tawed bindings
  RT   Fur bindings
        Leather bindings >
        Vellum bindings

Alum tawed thongs
  BT   Thongs

Aluminum bindings

Antique bindings
  USE   Retrospective bindings

Apollo and Pegasus bindings
  UF   Canevari bindings

Architectural bindings
  RT   Cathedral bindings

Armorial bindings
        [Bindings with a coat of arms, or any part of a coat of arms, e.g., a crest]
  UF   Heraldic bindings
  RT   Monogrammed bindings
        Royal bindings

Azured tools
  USE   Hatched tools

Backless bindings

Bands
   NT Disguised bands
       Double bands
       False bands
       Raised bands
   RT Cords >
       Tapes >
       Thongs >

Bevelled edge boards
   UF Chamfered edge boards
   RT Square edge boards

Bills, Binders'
   USE Binders' bills

Binders' bills
   UF Bills, Binders'

Binders' instructions
   UF Instructions, Binders'

Binders' receipts
   UF Receipts, Binders'

Binders' tickets
   UF Tickets, Binders'
   RT Signed bindings

Binding errors
      [For any kind of errors in binding, except folding errors]
   UF Errors in binding
   RT Folding errors

Binding labels
   USE Labels

Blind rolled bindings
   USE Blind tooled bindings

Blind stamped bindings
   USE Blind tooled bindings

Blind tooled bindings
> UF Blind rolled bindings
> Blind stamped bindings
> RT Gold tooled bindings
> Platinum tooled bindings
> Silver tooled bindings

Block printed papers
> USE Woodblock printed papers

Blocked bindings
> UF Panel stamps
> Plaque-impressed bindings
> NT Gold blocked bindings

Boards
> NT Hemp boards
> Pasteboard
> Wooden boards >

Book jackets
> USE Dust jackets

Bookbinding
> [Use only with subdivisions, to identify noteworthy binding types, styles, and techniques which cannot be otherwise classified using terms on this list]

Bosses
> BT Furniture
> NT Brass bosses

Braided headbands
> USE Plaited headbands

Brass bosses
> BT Bosses

Brass clasps
> BT Metal clasps

Brocade bindings
> UF Silk brocade bindings
> BT Cloth bindings

Buntpapier
> USE Decorated papers

Bust rolls
    USE   Medallion tools

Bust stamps
    USE   Medallion tools

Buttonhole stitched headbands
    BT   Worked headbands

Calf bindings
    BT   Leather bindings

Cameo rolls
    USE   Medallion tools

Cameo stamps
    USE   Medallion tools

Canevari bindings
    USE   Apollo and Pegasus bindings

Caoutchouc bindings
    UF   Gutta percha bindings
    BT   Adhesive bindings

Case bindings

Catches
    UF   Pins
    NT   Silver catches
    RT   Clasp plates >
         Clasps >
         Loop-and-ball fastenings
         Ties >

Cathedral bindings
    RT   Architectural bindings

Centerpiece and cornerpiece bindings
    RT   Centerpieces (Designs)
         Cornerpieces (Designs)

Centerpieces (Designs)
    RT   Centerpiece and cornerpiece bindings
         Cornerpieces (Designs)

Centerpieces (Furniture)
    BT   Furniture
    RT   Cornerpieces (Furniture)

Chained bindings
    RT   Furniture >

Chamfered edge boards
    USE   Bevelled edge boards

Chemises

Circuit edges
    RT   Flap bindings
          Yapp style bindings

Clasp plates
    NT   Silver clasp plates
    RT   Catches >
          Clasps >

Clasps
    NT   Enamel clasps
          Metal clasps >
    RT   Catches >
          Clasp plates >
          Loop-and-ball fastenings
          Ties >

Cloth bindings
        [Not for publishers' cloth; primarily for 16th-17th century bindings covered in
           cloth]
    UF   Textile bindings
    NT   Brocade bindings
          Embroidered bindings
          Lace bindings (Materials)
          Needlepoint bindings >
          Velvet bindings
    RT   Publishers' cloth bindings >

Cloth labels
    BT   Labels

Cloth tapes
    BT   Tapes

Cloth wrappers
    UF   Printed cloth wrappers
    BT   Wrappers

Contemporary bindings
    RT   Original covers
         Publishers' bindings >

Coptic bindings

Cords
    NT   Double cords
         Raised cords
         Recessed cords
    RT   Bands >
         Tapes >
         Thongs >

Cornerpieces (Designs)
    RT   Centerpiece and cornerpiece bindings
         Centerpieces (Designs)

Cornerpieces (Furniture)
    BT   Furniture
    RT   Centerpieces (Furniture)

Cosway bindings

Cottage style bindings

Cottonian Library book covers
         [Robert Southey's cloth book covers]

Cuir bouilli bindings
    USE   Molded leather bindings

Cuir-ciselé bindings
         ["Cuir-ciselé or cut-leather is a self-explanatory decorative technique: the leather is
             given patterns inscribed by a knife or other sharp tool."--Needham]
    UF   Cut leather bindings
         Lederschnitt bindings

Cut leather bindings
    USE   Cuir-ciselé bindings

Cutout leatherwork
    USE   Tracery

Decorated edges
  UF Edge decoration
  NT Gauffered edges
      Gilt edges
      Graphite edges
      Painted edges >
      Paste edges
      Stained edges >

Decorated papers
      [Use for the occurrence of such papers as any part of bindings, cases, endpapers, or
        doublures]
  UF Buntpapier
      Patterned papers
  NT Embossed papers >
      Flock papers
      Marbled papers
      Painted papers
      Paste papers
      Printed papers >
      Sprinkled papers
      Stamped papers
      Stencilled papers

Dentelle bindings
  UF Lace bindings (Designs)

Diced leather bindings

Disguised bands
  BT Bands

Dos-à-dos bindings

Double bands
  BT Bands

Double cords
  BT Cords

Double fore-edge paintings
  BT Fore-edge paintings

Double leaf format
  USE Accordion fold format

Doublures
   NT Leather doublures >
        Moiré doublures
        Silk doublures
        Tooled doublures
        Vellum doublures

Dust jackets
       [A detachable flexible cover (usually paper) for a book. Cf. Wrappers]
   UF Book jackets
        Dust wrappers

Dust wrappers
   USE Dust jackets

Dutch flowered papers
   USE Dutch gilt papers

✓ Dutch gilt papers *(Newberry cat : 9/94)*
   UF Dutch flowered papers
   BT Embossed papers

Edge decoration
   USE Decorated edges

Edge titles
       [The identification of the author, title, etc. of a book written on the edge of its
          block]
   UF Fore-edge titles
   RT Labels >
        Tooled lettering

Edges, Untrimmed
   USE Untrimmed edges

Embossed bindings
   NT Embossed cloth bindings

Embossed cloth bindings
   BT Embossed bindings
        Publishers' cloth bindings

Embossed papers
   BT Decorated papers
   NT Dutch gilt papers

Embroidered bindings
    UF   Needlework bindings
    BT   Cloth bindings

Enamel bindings
    UF   Limoges work bindings
    BT   Treasure bindings

Enamel clasps
    BT   Clasps

Endbands
    USE   Headbands

Endpapers
    UF   Lining papers
    RT   Vellum endleaves

Engraved paper labels
    BT   Paper labels

Errors in binding
    USE   Binding errors

Errors in folding
    USE   Folding errors

Etruscan bindings
        [An English binding style used from the 1770s through the first few decades of the nineteenth century. Characterized by an outer border of palmettes created by acid staining, and a central panel which is usually tree calf]

Fabric ties
    USE   Ties

False bands
    BT   Bands

Fan style bindings
    NT   Scottish wheel design bindings

Fanfare bindings

Filigree
        [Decorative work using fine wires, usually gold or silver. Use for filigree occurring anywhere on bindings or casings]

Fillet tools
    UF Roulette tools
    RT Gouge tools
         Pallet tools

Flap bindings
    UF Flaps
         Wallet edges
    RT Circuit edges
         Tucks
         Yapp style bindings

Flaps
    USE Flap bindings

Flat spines
    USE Smooth spines

Flock papers
    BT Decorated papers

Folding errors
        [For errors in folding one or more sheets of text]
    UF Errors in folding
    RT Binding errors

Fore-edge paintings
    BT Painted edges
    NT Double fore-edge paintings

Fore-edge titles
    USE Edge titles

French pointillé tooling
    USE Pointillé tooling

Fur bindings
    RT Alum tawed bindings
         Leather bindings >
         Vellum bindings

Furniture
        [Metal attachments to one or both covers. Their function is to protect the binding]
    UF   Metal furniture
    NT   Bosses >
         Centerpieces (Furniture)
         Cornerpieces (Furniture)
         Silver furniture
    RT   Chained bindings

Gauffered edges
    UF   Goffered edges
         Tooled edges
    BT   Decorated edges

Gem bindings
    USE   Jewelled bindings

Geometric rolls
    USE   Geometric tools

Geometric stamps
    USE   Geometric tools

Geometric tools
    UF   Geometric rolls
         Geometric stamps
    RT   Vegetal tools
         Zoomorphic tools

Gilt blocked bindings
    USE   Gold blocked bindings

Gilt edges
    BT   Decorated edges

Gilt silver bindings
    USE   Silver bindings

Girdle books

Glued-on headbands
    USE   Stuck-on headbands

Goatskin bindings
    BT   Leather bindings
    NT   Morocco bindings

Goffered edges
   USE   Gauffered edges

Gold blocked bindings
         [Bindings with a design impressed by a block through gold.]
   UF   Gilt blocked bindings
   BT   Blocked bindings

Gold powdered bindings

Gold stamped bindings
   USE   Gold tooled bindings

Gold tooled bindings
         ["Gold tooling--the bonding of gold leaf to leather by means of heated
            stamps."--Needham]
   UF   Gold stamped bindings
   RT   Blind tooled bindings
         Platinum tooled bindings
         Silver tooled bindings

Gouge tools
   RT   Fillet tools
         Pallet tools

Graphite edges
   BT   Decorated edges

Greek style bindings
         ["Points of this fashion include the use of wooden boards, with grooved edges;
            smooth backs, with no bands showing through; raised headcaps at top and bottom
            of the back, containing a double row of sewn headbands; edges of the leaves cut
            flush with the boards; clasps made of braided leather, catching on pins protruding
            from the edge of the boards of the upper covers."--Needham]

Grotesque bindings
         [16th century; decorated with grotesque figures, usually classical]

Guard books
   UF   Stub books

Guards
   UF   Sewing strips

Gutta percha bindings
   USE   Caoutchouc bindings

Half bindings
    RT   Quarter bindings
          Three-quarter bindings

Hatched tools
    UF   Azured tools
    RT   Open tools
          Solid tools

Headbands
    UF   Endbands
    NT   Stuck-on headbands
          Worked headbands >

Headcaps

Hemp boards
    BT   Boards

Heraldic bindings
    USE   Armorial bindings

Hollis bindings

Hollow backs
    RT   Tight backs

Inlays
    RT   Onlays

Instructions, Binders'
    USE   Binders' instructions

Interlace bindings
    UF   Strapwork bindings

Iron clasps
    BT   Metal clasps

Islamic bindings
    RT   Mudéjar bindings

Ivory bindings
    BT   Treasure bindings

Jansenist style bindings

Japanese sewing

Jewelled bindings
 UF Gem bindings
 BT Treasure bindings

Kermes dyed bindings
   [Bindings dyed by means of Kermes (a red dyestuff obtained from a Mediterranean scale insect). Kermes was largely supplanted by cochineal as a dyestuff after the latter's introduction into Europe in the 16th and 17th centuries]

Labels
 UF Binding labels
   Spine labels
 NT Cloth labels
   Lettering pieces
   Paper labels >
 RT Edge titles
   Tooled lettering

Lace bindings (Designs)
 USE Dentelle bindings

Lace bindings (Materials)
 UF Needlework bindings
 BT Cloth bindings

Lacquered bindings
   [Bindings with scenes on their covers which are first painted and then covered with lacquer. Primarily 16th century; the painted scenes can be on leather or pasteboard]
 RT Painted bindings >

Lambskin bindings
 BT Sheepskin bindings

Landscape bindings

Law bindings

Leather bindings
    NT Calf bindings
           Goatskin bindings >
           Pigskin bindings
           Russia leather bindings
           Shagreen bindings
           Sheepskin bindings >
    RT Alum tawed bindings
           Fur bindings
           Vellum bindings

Leather doublures
    BT Doublures
    NT Morocco doublures
           Suede doublures

Leather labels
    USE Lettering pieces

Leather thongs
    BT Thongs

Lederschnitt bindings
    USE Cuir-ciselé bindings

Ledger bindings

Letter pieces
    USE Lettering pieces

Lettering pieces
    UF Leather labels
          Letter pieces
          Skiver labels
    BT Labels

Levant bindings
    USE Morocco bindings

Limoges work bindings
    USE Enamel bindings

Limp bindings
       [Use for any kind of limp binding]
    RT Wrappers >

Lining papers
    USE Endpapers

Linings
    UF   Spine linings

Loop-and-ball fastenings
    RT   Catches >
          Clasps >
          Ties >

Mahogany marbled calf bindings
    USE Tree calf bindings

Manuscript waste
    BT   Waste

Marbled calf bindings
    NT Tree calf bindings
    RT Stained calf bindings

Marbled edges
    BT   Stained edges

Marbled inlaid leather
    USE Maril

Marbled papers
    BT   Decorated papers

Maril
    UF   Marbled inlaid leather

Masonic bindings
        [Bindings decorated with masonic motifs; primarily late 18th and early 19th
           centuries]

Medallion rolls
    USE Medallion tools

Medallion stamps
    USE Medallion tools

Medallion tools
  UF   Bust rolls
       Bust stamps
       Cameo rolls
       Cameo stamps
       Medallion rolls
       Medallion stamps
       Portrait medallion rolls
       Portrait medallion stamps

Medieval treasure bindings
  USE   Treasure bindings

Metal clasps
  BT   Clasps
  NT   Brass clasps
       Iron clasps
       Silver clasps

Metal furniture
  USE   Furniture

Middle Hill boards
       [Found on books and manuscripts bound for Sir Thomas Phillipps' library at Middle
       Hill. The usual style is drab colored paper over millboard, without pastedowns or
       other endpapers. The text block is sewn on two cords which are laced through the
       boards. Phillipps' shelf-mark is usually present in the form: [Roman
       numeral].[lower case letter].[Arabic numeral]]

Moiré doublures
  BT   Doublures

Molded leather bindings
  UF   Cuir bouilli bindings
       Sculptured leather bindings
       Shaped leather bindings

Monogrammed bindings
  RT   Armorial bindings
       Royal bindings

Morocco bindings
  UF   Levant bindings
  BT   Goatskin bindings

Morocco doublures
  BT   Leather doublures

Mosaic bindings

Mottled calf bindings
  RT   Stained calf bindings

Mudéjar bindings
       [A Spanish binding style, used in the 13th-15th centuries, "with Islamic decorative
         schemes: elaborate geometric interlace bands against a background entirely filled
         with hundreds of repetitions of small knotwork or cablework tools."--Needham]
  RT   Islamic bindings

Needlepoint bindings
  UF   Needlework bindings
  BT   Cloth bindings
  NT   Petit point bindings

Needlework bindings
  USE   Embroidered bindings
         Lace bindings (Materials)
         Needlepoint bindings

Non-adhesive bindings
  RT   Adhesive bindings >

Onlays
  RT   Inlays

Open tools
  RT   Hatched tools
        Solid tools

Original covers
       [For examples of original covers as issued by the bookseller, publisher, etc.]
  RT   Contemporary bindings
        Publishers' bindings >

Orihon format
  USE   Accordion fold format

Overcasting

Painted bindings
  NT   Painted leather bindings
        Vellucent bindings
  RT   Lacquered bindings

Painted edges
    BT   Decorated edges
    NT   Fore-edge paintings >

Painted leather bindings
    BT   Painted bindings
    RT   Stained calf bindings

Painted papers
    BT   Decorated papers

Pallet tools
    RT   Fillet tools
          Gouge tools

Panel stamps
    USE   Blocked bindings

Paper bindings
    RT   Publishers' paper bindings

Paper labels
    BT   Labels
    NT   Engraved paper labels
          Printed paper labels

Paper wrappers
    USE   Wrappers

Papier-mâché bindings

Parchment bindings
    USE   Vellum bindings

Paste edges
    BT   Decorated edges

Paste papers
    BT   Decorated papers

Pasteboard
    BT   Boards

Patterned papers
    USE   Decorated papers

Peccary bindings
    USE   Pigskin bindings

Penitential bindings
["A number of later sixteenth-century Parisian 'penitential' bindings are tooled in silver on dark brown morocco to create a somber appearance."--Needham]
RT   Somber bindings

Perfect bindings
USE   Adhesive bindings

Petit point bindings
BT   Needlepoint bindings

Pictorial bindings

Pictorial cloth bindings
BT   Publishers' cloth bindings

Pictorial paper wrappers
USE   Printed wrappers

Pigskin bindings
UF   Peccary bindings
BT   Leather bindings

Pinhead style bindings
RT   Pointillé tooling

Pins
USE   Catches

Plaited headbands
UF   Braided headbands
BT   Worked headbands

Plaque-impressed bindings
USE   Blocked bindings

Plaquette stamps

Platina tooled bindings
USE   Platinum tooled bindings

Platinum tooled bindings
UF   Platina tooled bindings
RT   Blind tooled bindings
     Gold tooled bindings
     Silver tooled bindings

Pointillé tooling
    UF   French pointillé tooling
    RT   Pinhead style bindings

Portrait medallion rolls
    USE   Medallion tools

Portrait medallion stamps
    USE   Medallion tools

Presentation bindings

Printed boards
    BT   Publishers' bindings

Printed cloth wrappers
    USE   Cloth wrappers

Printed paper labels *(Newberry cat; 9/94)*
    BT   Paper labels

Printed paper wrappers
    USE   Printed wrappers

Printed papers
    BT   Decorated papers
    NT   Woodblock printed papers

Printed waste
    BT   Waste

Printed wrappers
    UF   Pictorial paper wrappers
          Printed paper wrappers
    BT   Wrappers

Prize bindings

Publishers' bindings
    NT   Printed boards
          Publishers' cloth bindings >
          Publishers' paper bindings
    RT   Contemporary bindings
          Original covers

Publishers' cloth bindings
    BT   Publishers' bindings
    NT   Embossed cloth bindings
           Pictorial cloth bindings
    RT   Cloth bindings >

Publishers' paper bindings
    BT   Publishers' bindings
    RT   Paper bindings

Punch-dotting
       ["A type of decoration of Islamic origin in which small punched depressions in the leather are filled with a kind of colored gesso."--Needham]

Quarter bindings
    RT   Half bindings
           Three-quarter bindings

Raised bands
    BT   Bands

Raised cords
    BT   Cords

Rebacking

Recasing

Receipts, Binders'
    USE   Binders' receipts

Recessed cords
    UF   Sawn-in cords
    BT   Cords

Red ruling
    USE   Ruling in red

Remboîtage

Repoussé silver bindings
    USE   Silver bindings

Resewing

Retrospective bindings
       [A conscious imitation of an earlier style]
    UF   Antique bindings

Reversed leather bindings

Roan bindings
    UF   Split sheepskin bindings
    BT   Sheepskin bindings

Roulette tools
    USE   Fillet tools

Royal bindings
    RT   Armorial bindings
          Monogrammed bindings

Ruling in red
          [Manuscript ruling in red ink in order to set off the text]
    UF   Red ruling

Russia calf bindings
    USE   Russia leather bindings

Russia leather bindings
    UF   Russia calf bindings
    BT   Leather bindings

Sawn-in cords
    USE   Recessed cords

Scaleboard
    BT   Wooden boards

Scottish herringbone design bindings
    RT   Scottish wheel design bindings

Scottish wheel design bindings
    BT   Fan style bindings
    RT   Scottish herringbone design bindings

Sculptured leather bindings
    USE   Molded leather bindings

Semé

Settle bindings

Sewing strips
    USE   Guards

Shagreen bindings
    BT   Leather bindings

Shaped leather bindings
    USE   Molded leather bindings

Sheepskin bindings
    BT   Leather bindings
    NT   Lambskin bindings
          Roan bindings

Signed bindings
    RT   Binders' tickets

Silk brocade bindings
    USE   Brocade bindings

Silk doublures
    BT   Doublures

Silk ties
    BT   Ties

Silver bindings
    UF   Gilt silver bindings
          Repoussé silver bindings
    BT   Treasure bindings

Silver catches
    BT   Catches
    RT   Silver clasp plates
          Silver clasps

Silver clasp plates
    BT   Clasp plates
    RT   Silver catches
          Silver clasps

Silver clasps
    BT   Metal clasps
    RT   Silver catches
          Silver clasp plates

Silver furniture
    BT   Furniture

Silver tooled bindings
    RT   Blind tooled bindings
          Gold tooled bindings
          Platinum tooled bindings

Skiver labels
    USE Lettering pieces

Smooth spines
    UF Flat spines

Solid tools
    RT   Hatched tools
          Open tools

Somber bindings
        ["'Somber' bindings of silver-tooled black morocco were common in Restoration
          England." –Needham]
    RT   Penitential bindings

Spine labels
    USE Labels

Spine linings
    USE Linings

Split sheepskin bindings
    USE Roan bindings

Sprinkled calf bindings
    RT   Stained calf bindings

Sprinkled edges
    BT   Stained edges

Sprinkled papers
    BT   Decorated papers

Square edge boards
    RT   Bevelled edge boards

Stabbing

Stained calf bindings
[Use for leather stained in ways other than by marbling, mottling, or sprinkling. This includes staining by means of blocking, stencilling, or free-hand design]
RT   Marbled calf bindings >
Mottled calf bindings
Painted leather bindings
Sprinkled calf bindings

Stained edges
BT   Decorated edges
NT   Marbled edges
Sprinkled edges

Stained vellum bindings

Stamped papers
BT   Decorated papers

Stencilled papers
BT   Decorated papers

Strapwork bindings
USE   Interlace bindings

Stub books
USE   Guard books

Stuck-on headbands
UF   Glued-on headbands
BT   Headbands

Suede doublures
BT   Leather doublures

Tall copies
RT   Untrimmed edges

Tapes
NT   Cloth tapes
Vellum tapes
RT   Bands >
Cords >
Thongs >

Textile bindings
USE   Cloth bindings

Thongs
  NT Alum tawed thongs
      Leather thongs
      Vellum thongs
  RT Bands >
      Cords >
      Tapes >

Three-quarter bindings
  RT Half bindings
      Quarter bindings

Tickets, Binders'
  USE Binders' tickets

Ties
  UF Fabric ties
  NT Silk ties
  RT Catches >
      Clasps >
      Loop-and-ball fastenings

Tight backs
  RT Hollow backs

Tooled doublures
  BT Doublures

Tooled edges
  USE Gauffered edges

Tooled lettering
  UF Tooled titles
  RT Edge titles
      Labels >

Tooled titles
  USE Tooled lettering

Tortoise shell bindings

Tracery
      ["Cutout leatherwork, or tracery, was never a common technique in European
      bookbinding, but examples are known from the fifteenth and sixteenth centuries ...
      Several of the earliest European gold-tooled bookbindings, from both Venice and
      Naples, have leather tracery decoration, which was brought out, as in the Islamic
      archetypes, by being laid over a bright azure ground."--Needham]
  UF Cutout leatherwork

Treasure bindings
> ["Covered with gold and silver, ivories, enamelwork, and gems."--Needham]

UF Medieval treasure bindings
NT Enamel bindings
      Ivory bindings
      Jewelled bindings
      Silver bindings

Tree calf bindings
UF Mahogany marbled calf bindings
BT Marbled calf bindings
RT Tree sheep bindings

Tree sheep bindings
> [In case of doubt use Tree calf bindings]

RT Tree calf bindings

Tucks
RT Flap bindings

Turn-ins

Two-on sewing
RT All along sewing

✓ Unbound sheets (5/16/90)

✓ Unopened books (5/16/90)
> [Books in which the folded edges of the sections have not been trimmed away or opened by a utensil such as a knife]

Untrimmed edges
UF Edges, Untrimmed
RT Tall copies

Vegetal rolls
USE Vegetal tools

Vegetal stamps
USE Vegetal tools

Vegetal tools
UF Vegetal rolls
      Vegetal stamps
RT Geometric tools
      Zoomorphic tools

Vellucent bindings
  BT Painted bindings

Vellum bindings
  UF Parchment bindings
  RT Alum tawed bindings
       Fur bindings
       Leather bindings >

Vellum doublures
  BT Doublures

Vellum endleaves
  RT Endpapers

Vellum pastedowns

Vellum tapes
  BT Tapes

Vellum thongs
  BT Thongs

Vellum wrappers
  BT Wrappers

Velvet bindings
  BT Cloth bindings

Wallet edges
  USE Flap bindings

Washing

Waste
  NT Manuscript waste
       Printed waste

Woodblock printed papers (Newberry cat: 9/94)
  UF Block printed papers
  BT Printed papers

Wooden bindings
  RT Wooden boards >

Wooden boards
    BT   Boards
    NT   Scaleboard
    RT   Wooden bindings

Worked headbands
    BT   Headbands
    NT   Buttonhole stitched headbands
          Plaited headbands

Wrappers
        [A physically attached flexible cover for a book. Cf. Dust jacket]
    UF   Paper wrappers
    NT   Cloth wrappers
          Printed wrappers
          Vellum wrappers
    RT   Limp bindings

Yapp style bindings
    RT   Circuit edges
          Flap bindings

Zoomorphic rolls
    USE   Zoomorphic tools

Zoomorphic stamps
    USE   Zoomorphic tools

Zoomorphic tools
    UF   Zoomorphic rolls
          Zoomorphic stamps
    RT   Geometric tools
          Vegetal tools

BINDING TERMS HIERARCHY

1. [Text block]
   Accordion fold format
   [Edges of text block]
       Decorated edges
           Gauffered edges
           Gilt edges
           Graphite edges
           Painted edges
               Fore-edge paintings
                   Double fore-edge paintings
           Paste edges
           Stained edges
               Marbled edges
               Sprinkled edges
       Untrimmed edges
   Ruling in red
   [Sewing patterns]
       All along sewing
       Stabbing
       Two-on sewing
       [Unsupported sewing]
           Japanese sewing
           Overcasting
   Tall copies
   Unbound sheets
   Unopened books

2. [Types of binding structure]
   Adhesive bindings
       Caoutchouc bindings
   Backless bindings
   Boards
       [Edges of binding boards]
           Bevelled edge boards
           Square edge boards
       Hemp boards
       Pasteboard
       Wooden boards
           Scaleboard
   Case bindings
   Circuit edges
   Dos-à-dos bindings
   Flap bindings
   Girdle books
   Guard books

Limp bindings
Non-adhesive bindings
Tucks
Wrappers
    Cloth wrappers
    Printed wrappers
    Vellum wrappers
Yapp style bindings

3.   [Supports]
Bands
    Disguised bands
    Double bands
    False bands
    Raised bands
Cords
    Double cords
    Raised cords
    Recessed cords
Guards
Tapes
    Cloth tapes
    Vellum tapes
Thongs
    Alum tawed thongs
    Leather thongs
    Vellum thongs

4.   [Spines]
Headcaps
Hollow backs
Linings
Smooth spines
Tight backs

5.   [Ancillary structures]
Doublures
    Leather doublures
        Morocco doublures
        Suede doublures
    Moiré doublures
    Silk doublures
    Tooled doublures
    Vellum doublures
Endpapers
Headbands
    Stuck-on headbands
    Worked headbands

Buttonhole stitched headbands
Plaited headbands
Turn-ins
Vellum endleaves
Vellum pastedowns

6.   [Materials and treatment]
Alum tawed bindings
Aluminum bindings
Cloth bindings
Brocade bindings
Embroidered bindings
Lace bindings (Materials)
Needlepoint bindings
Petit point bindings
Velvet bindings
Decorated papers
Embossed papers
Dutch gilt papers
Flock papers
Marbled papers
Painted papers
Paste papers
Printed papers
Woodblock printed papers
Sprinkled papers
Stamped papers
Stencilled papers
Embossed bindings
Embossed cloth bindings
Filigree
Fur bindings
Gold powdered bindings
Half bindings
Inlays
Kermes dyed bindings
Lacquered bindings
Leather bindings
Calf bindings
Marbled calf bindings
Tree calf bindings
Mottled calf bindings
Sprinkled calf bindings
Stained calf bindings
Cuir-ciselé bindings
Diced leather bindings
Goatskin bindings
Morocco bindings

Molded leather bindings
Pigskin bindings
Reversed leather bindings
Russia leather bindings
Shagreen bindings
Sheepskin bindings
 Lambskin bindings
 Roan bindings
 Tree sheep bindings
Maril
Onlays
Painted bindings
 Painted leather bindings
 Vellucent bindings
Paper bindings
Papier-mâché bindings
Pictorial cloth bindings
Printed boards
Quarter bindings
[Stamped or tooled bindings]
 Blind tooled bindings
 Blocked bindings
  Gold blocked bindings
 Gold tooled bindings
 Pinhead style bindings
 Platinum tooled bindings
 Pointillé tooling
 Punch-dotting
 Semé
 Silver tooled bindings
 [Types of tools]
  Fillet tools
  Geometric tools
  Gouge tools
  Hatched tools
  Medallion tools
  Open tools
  Pallet tools
  Plaquette stamps
  Solid tools
  Vegetal tools
  Zoomorphic tools
Three-quarter bindings
Tortoise shell bindings
Tracery
Treasure bindings
 Enamel bindings
 Ivory bindings

        Jewelled bindings
        Silver bindings
    Vellum bindings
        Stained vellum bindings
    Waste
        Manuscript waste
        Printed waste
    Wooden bindings

7.   [Fastenings, Attachments, or Titling]
    [Board fastenings]
        Catches
            Silver catches
        Clasp plates
            Silver clasp plates
        Clasps
            Enamel clasps
            Metal clasps
                Brass clasps
                Iron clasps
                Silver clasps
        Loop-and-ball fastenings
        Ties
            Silk ties
    Chained bindings
    Furniture
        Bosses
            Brass bosses
        Centerpieces (Furniture)
        Cornerpieces (Furniture)
        Silver furniture
    [Titling]
        Edge titles
        Labels
            Cloth labels
            Lettering pieces
            Paper labels
                Engraved paper labels
                Printed paper labels
        Tooled lettering

8.   [Protective housing]
    Chemises
    Dust jackets

9.   [Categories of bindings/Occasions for binding]
    Contemporary bindings
    Original covers

Presentation bindings
Prize bindings
[Proprietary bindings]
    Apollo and Pegasus bindings
    Armorial bindings
    Cottonian Library book covers
    Hollis bindings
    Middle Hill boards
    Monogrammed bindings
    Royal bindings
    Settle bindings
Publishers' bindings
    Publishers' cloth bindings
    Publishers' paper bindings

10. [Styles]

All-over style bindings
Architectural bindings
Cathedral bindings
Centerpiece and cornerpiece bindings
Centerpieces (Designs)
Coptic bindings
Cornerpieces (Designs)
Cosway bindings
Cottage style bindings
Dentelle bindings
Etruscan bindings
Fan style bindings
    Scottish wheel design bindings
Fanfare bindings
Greek style bindings
Grotesque bindings
Interlace bindings
Islamic bindings
Jansenist style bindings
Landscape bindings
Law bindings
Ledger bindings
Masonic bindings
Mosaic bindings
Mudéjar bindings
Penitential bindings
Pictorial bindings
Retrospective bindings
Scottish herringbone design bindings
Somber bindings

11. [Binders' evidence]

Binders' bills
Binders' instructions
Binders' receipts
Binders' tickets
Signed bindings

12. [Errors]
Binding errors
Folding errors

13. [Subsequent treatment]
Rebacking
Recasing
Remboîtage
Resewing
Washing